THEY DON'T BELONG

TRACKING INVASIVE SPECIES

Feral Pigs

Chomp, Chomp!

by Kevin Blake

Consultant: Tyler A. Campbell, PhD
Principal Scientist
East Foundation
San Antonio, Texas

BEARPORT
PUBLISHING

New York, New York

Credits

Cover and Title Page, © taviphoto/Shutterstock and © Bronwyn Photo/Shutterstock; 4, © groveb/iStock; 4B, © oliale72/iStock; 5, © Laurie L. Snidow/Shutterstock; 6, © North Wind Picture Archives/Alamy; 7T, © davemhuntphotography/Shutterstock; 7B, © Tsekhmister/Shutterstock; 8T, © Volodymyr Burdiak/ Shutterstock; 8B, © Antagain/iStockphoto; 9, © Eduard Kyslynskyy/Shutterstock; 10T, © Denis Pepin/Shutterstock; 10B, © Katoosha/Shutterstock; 11, © Vetapi/Shutterstock; 12, © Buiten-Beeld/Alamy; 13T, © Geoff Kuchera/ iStockphoto; 13B, © C.O. Mercial/Alamy; 14, © Neil Burton/Shutterstock; 15, © Rolf Nussbaumer Photography/ Alamy; 16T, troy mckaskle/tinyurl.com/mwp6eqh/CC-BY-SA-2.0; 16B, Forest & Kim Starr/tinyurl.com/lxmosql/ CC-BY-3.0; 17T, © travelpixpro/iStockphoto; 17B, Les Williams/tinyurl.com/lrvmpqm/CC-BY-SA-2.0; 18, U.S. Department of Agriculture/tinyurl.com/mzr7emx/CC-BY-2.0; 19, © Shannon Beineke/Shutterstock; 19B, © Laurie L. Snidow/Shutterstock; 20, © GeNik/Shutterstock; 21, © zimindmitry/iStockphoto; 22, © Texas A&M AgriLife Extension Service and Billy Higginbotham; 23, © Texas A&M AgriLife Extension Service and Billy Higginbotham; 24, © John Carnemolla/Shutterstock; 24T, © AP Photo/Eric Gay; 25, © Alexander Raths/Shutterstock; 26, VSPYCC/ tinyurl.com/loo3em2/CC-BY-2.0; 27, © Eduard Kyslynskyy/Shutterstock; 28T, Chung Bill Bill/tinyurl.com/l39ucel/ CC-BY-2.0; 28B, © Eduard Kyslynskyy/Shutterstock; 29T, © MikeLane45/iStockphoto; 29B, © Malyshev Oleg/ Shutterstock.

Publisher: Kenn Goin
Senior Editor: Joyce Tavolacci
Creative Director: Spencer Brinker
Design: Dawn Beard Creative
Photo Researcher: Jennifer Zeiger

Library of Congress Cataloging-in-Publication Data

Blake, Kevin, 1978– author.
  Feral pigs : chomp, chomp! / by Kevin Blake.
    pages cm. — (They don't belong : tracking invasive species)
  Includes bibliographical references and index.
  ISBN 978-1-62724-829-7 (library binding) — ISBN 1-62724-829-3 (library binding)
  1. Feral swine—Juvenile literature. 2. Pest introduction—Juvenile literature. 3. Nonindigenous pests—Juvenile literature. 4. Nature—Effect of human beings on—Juvenile literature. [1. Pigs.] I. Title.
  SF397.8.B53 2016
  599.63'3—dc23
                                    2015011062

For more information, write to Bearport Publishing Company, Inc., 45 West 21st Street, Suite 3B, New York, New York 10010. Printed in the United States of America.

10 9 8 7 6 5 4 3 2 1

Contents

Living Bulldozers

On a warm summer evening in 2012, the sun set over a large cornfield in upstate New York. Neatly planted corn swayed in the night breeze. When the sun rose the next day, however, the field was destroyed. Half-eaten corn hung from broken stalks. Huge **craters** dotted the field. It looked like powerful bulldozers had plowed through the soil in the middle of the night.

A cornfield

Damaged corn

When **biologist** Ed Reed arrived at the farm to view the damage, he immediately knew that machines had not caused it. Rather, it was a family of hungry 200-pound (91 kg) animals with short **tusks** and hairy bodies. This was the work of **feral** pigs!

Feral pigs are also known as wild pigs.

The average adult male feral pig weighs about 200 pounds (91 kg). Adult females typically weigh 175 pounds (79 kg). Occasionally, a feral pig will reach more than 300 pounds (136 kg).

Arriving by Ship

Hundreds of years ago, there were no pigs in North America. That's because pigs are **native** to Europe and Asia. However, in 1539, an explorer named Hernando de Soto sailed from Spain to what is now Florida and brought about a dozen **domesticated** pigs with him. The pigs, which were raised for food, multiplied quickly. Because they were not kept in pens, many of the pigs escaped into the wild.

This illustration shows Hernando de Soto and his men setting up camp in what is now Florida.

Hernando de Soto brought pigs from Spain to North America.

In the 1600s and 1700s, early American settlers also kept domesticated pigs for food. Some of these pigs escaped as well. By the 1800s, thousands of feral pigs were scattered across the United States. Today, more than 200 years later, as many as 8 million feral pigs roam the country, all the way from New York to Hawaii—and their **population** is still growing.

A Eurasian wild boar

In the 1900s, Europeans brought Eurasian wild boars to parts of the United States. They released the boars into the wild and hunted them for sport. The wild boars had babies with the feral pigs already living in the United States, creating **hybrids**. Today, hybrid pigs make up part of the population of wild pigs.

Domesticated pigs

Live Anywhere, Eat Anything

How did the wild pig population grow into the millions, and why does it keep increasing? One reason is that wild pigs can live almost anywhere. They have been found in as many as 44 states—living everywhere from dry Texas grasslands to wet Florida swamps.

Feral pigs can live anywhere as long as they have access to water to drink and to cool off in.

Wild pigs sometimes make their homes on sandy beaches.

In addition to being able to live in many different **habitats**, feral pigs will **devour** almost anything. They are **omnivores** that eat roots, seeds such as acorns, and other plant parts, as well as meat. Although plants make up 90 percent of their diet, the pigs also gobble down worms, frogs, other small animals—and even **carrion**.

This wild pig is searching for food in a forest.

Wild pigs can consume up to 5 percent of their weight in a typical day—or about 10 pounds (4.5 kg) of food.

Piglets Everywhere

The population of feral pigs is growing for another important reason. Female pigs can have lots of babies. When they are only six months old, female pigs, called sows, can start to **breed**. Twice a year, sows can have as many as 8 new piglets—that's 16 babies each year!

A wild sow with her piglets

Baby feral pigs often have striped coats.

Females and their babies live in family groups called **sounders**. These groups may have as few as 6 pigs or as many as 100. Adult males usually live alone.

Animals such as owls, foxes, and coyotes sometimes hunt and eat the tiny piglets. However, adult wild pigs don't have many enemies. With few natural **predators**, feral pigs can quickly take over an **environment**. "They are the ultimate survivors," says biologist John Mayer.

A large adult male with tusks

Environmental Harm

The millions of feral pigs in the United States are having a huge impact on the environment. For example, when feral pigs devour the acorns of oak trees or other seeds in a forest, those seeds cannot become new plants. This can have a big effect on what kinds of plants grow in the forest.

These young pigs are eating acorns.

Because the pigs eat so many acorns and seeds, few are left for native wildlife such as deer and wild turkeys to eat. That means that these native animals might not have enough food to survive the winter.

White-tailed deer

Wild pigs rub their bodies on trees to remove ticks and other **parasites** from their skin. This can tear off the trees' bark and make the trees more likely to die.

The bark of this tree is being stripped away by a wild pig.

More Destruction

Wild pigs also dig up and destroy the land. Using their long snouts and sharp hooves, they **root** in the dirt, digging up plants, **tubers**, and underground animals to eat. Sometimes, they dig holes up to 3 feet (0.9 m) deep!

The long, powerful snouts of feral pigs can tear up the soil and kill plants.

In addition to their destructive digging, pigs roll around in mud to cool off. Over time, this creates huge muddy craters, or **wallows**, in the ground. The pigs also go to the bathroom in the water. The dirty water from pig wallows can seep into the ground or into nearby streams and pollute them.

A pig in its muddy wallow

A wild pig wallow can be the size of a large swimming pool.

Pigs in Paradise

One place in the United States that has a very serious pig problem is Hawaii. In certain areas, including some of the islands' rain forests, the pigs dig up plants and turn the soil into a muddy mess. While rooting for tasty ferns to eat on the forest floor, the wild pigs destroy rare plants such as certain kinds of **orchids** found only in Hawaii.

A feral pig in Hawaii

A Hawaiian orchid

Wild pigs were introduced to the Hawaiian Islands by **Polynesian** settlers more than 1,000 years ago.

The wild pigs are also a threat to Hawaii's birds. The pigs snack on birds' eggs and stomp on their nests. They also make huge wallows that attract insects like mosquitoes, which breed in pools of water. These mosquitoes, in turn, can spread diseases that are very dangerous to some birds.

Haleakalā National Park in Hawaii

To prevent wild pigs from entering and damaging Haleakalā National Park (above) on the Hawaiian island of Maui, the U.S. government has spent about $5 million to build a pig-proof fence.

Hawaiian birds called honeycreepers are dying from diseases carried by mosquitoes.

Messin' with Texas

Texas is another state with a huge pig problem. In fact, there may be more than three million wild pigs living there. That's almost half the total number of feral pigs in the country! Making matters worse, some experts think the population of wild pigs in Texas could double in as little as five years.

Feral pigs have become a nuisance across much of Texas. These pigs

The millions of feral pigs roaming around Texas cause up to $500 million in damage per year.

The pigs don't just stick to Texas's **rural** areas. In busy towns, people have spotted the pigs rooting up lawns, golf courses, and baseball fields. Wild pigs have already made themselves at home in Houston, the state's largest city. There are up to 15,000 of them living in Houston's George Bush Park.

A golf course in Texas

Run-Ins

With feral pigs wandering around cities and towns, it's not a surprise that people often spot them near their homes. In a suburb of Atlanta, Georgia, Taneisha Danner watched a huge feral pig dig through her garbage bins. "My children are even afraid to be downstairs, worried that (the pig) could come through the door," she says. Near Orlando, Florida, worried parents thought about canceling their 2014 Halloween celebrations because of the fear of a pig attack.

As the wild pig population grows, there will be more contact between people and pigs.

For the most part, feral pigs want to avoid encounters with people. "If they feel threatened, they can become aggressive, they can bite," says biologist Charlie Killmaster. "But in nearly all cases, steering clear of them is all you need to do."

Wild pigs sometimes wander onto roadways and are struck by cars.

A wild pig approaching a roadway

Trapped!

So what are people doing to control the growing number of wild pigs in the United States? Some farmers have placed **corral traps** in areas where they know wild pigs come to eat. They **bait** the large traps with corn and other foods that pigs love. Once the pigs go inside to feed, a door slams shut.

A corral trap used to catch wild pigs

The walls of a feral pig trap have to be at least 5 feet (1.5 m) high. Wild pigs can jump out of traps with lower walls. Pigs have also been known to stand on top of each other in order to escape traps.

Traps, however, don't always work. According to many scientists, feral pigs are incredibly smart. When wild pigs see their family members get trapped, they quickly learn how to avoid new traps. Even hungry feral pigs will pass up food if they think they are about to get captured.

Some feral pigs, like the ones shown here, have learned how to avoid getting trapped and how to escape traps.

Pig Control

Traps are just one way people try to keep the feral pig population under control. Hunters also trek into the woods with specially trained dogs to find and kill wild pigs. Other hunters have taken to the sky to shoot the animals from helicopters.

A hunter in Texas searches for feral pigs from a helicopter.

Hunters in Texas alone kill about 750,000 wild pigs a year. However, this is still not enough to prevent the feral pig population from growing.

Scientists are trying a different approach, however. Dr. Tatiana Samoylova and a team of researchers at Auburn University in Alabama are developing a drug that will prevent feral pigs from having more piglets. If fewer pigs are born, the pig population should drop.

Scientists are working to develop drugs that will prevent pigs from reproducing but will not harm other animals.

The Future

While scientists are working hard to address the pig problem, the animals continue to spread across the country and dig up the land. "Free-roaming wild pigs have become one of North America's most threatening invasive mammal species," according to experts at an organization called The Wildlife Society. Scientists worry that if they cannot control the population of wild pigs within the next ten years, they might never be able to control it.

This curious wild pig walks up to a group of people.

However, with the help of scientists and hunters, there is hope for reducing the number of feral pigs in the future. Texas wildlife expert Billy Higginbotham agrees: "We are not going to **eradicate** them; our hope is that we can reduce their population to reduce damage."

Feral pigs can move fast. At full speed, they can run up to 30 miles per hour (48 kph)— that's as fast as a car going down a city street!

Other Invasive Mammals

The feral pig is just one kind of mammal that has invaded the United States. Here are some others.

Black Rat

- The black rat came to North America aboard settlers' ships in the 1500s.

- While the rat will eat almost anything, it especially likes birds' eggs. The black rat is responsible for the **extinction** of many native birds in the United States.

- The black rat also spreads deadly diseases, such as the bubonic plague and typhus.

Feral Cat

- There are thought to be tens of millions of feral cats in the United Sates. In Florida alone, there are an estimated 5.3 million feral cats on the loose. Many of these are the young of escaped pets.

- These cats are great hunters. As a result, they are threatening populations of native mice, rabbits, and birds.

- Feral cats often live in large groups called colonies.

Nutria

- The nutria is a small mammal from South America. It spends much of its time in the water.

- People first brought the nutria to the United States because they wanted to harvest its fur, which is used to make coats and hats.

- The nutria eats plants that grow in wetlands. In places like Louisiana, native species are losing their habitat because of the nutria's big appetite.

Small Asian Mongoose

- The small Asian mongoose was brought to Hawaii from India to protect sugarcane from rats.

- The mongoose, however, has killed more than just rats. It has also killed many of Hawaii's native birds.

- The mongoose is less than 2 feet (0.6 m) long.

- It can start reproducing at four months old.

Glossary

bait (BAYT) to place food in a trap to attract an animal

biologist (bye-OL-uh-jist) a scientist who studies animals or plants

breed (BREED) to produce young

carrion (KA-ree-uhn) rotting meat

corral traps (kuh-RAHL trapz) circular traps used to capture animals

craters (KRAY-turz) large, round holes in the ground

devour (di-VOUR) to eat something quickly

domesticated (duh-MESS-tuh-*kayt*-id) having been tamed to be able to live closely with people

environment (en-VYE-ruhn-muhnt) the area where animals or plants live, and all the things, such as weather, that affect that place

eradicate (ih-RAD-uh-kate) to destroy completely

extinction (ek-STINGK-shun) when an animal or plant dies out

feral (FEH-ruhl) in a wild state

habitats (HAB-uh-*tats*) places in nature where a plant or an animal normally lives

hybrids (HYE-bridz) young that have been bred from two different kinds of animals

native (NAY-tiv) to have always lived in a place; to belong to a place

omnivores (AHM-ni-vohrz) animals that eat both plants and animals

orchids (OHR-kidz) plants that often have unusually shaped flowers

parasites (PA-ruh-*sites*) plants or animals that get food by living on or in another plant or animal

Polynesian (*pol*-uh-NEE-zhuhn) relating to islands in the Pacific Ocean or the people who live there

population (*pop*-yuh-LAY-shun) the total number of a kind of animal living in a place

predators (PRED-uh-turz) animals that hunt and eat other animals

root (ROOT) to dig up from the ground

rural (RUR-uhl) having to do with the countryside

sounders (SOWN-duhrz) large groups of pigs

tubers (TOO-buhrz) the thick, underground stems of certain plants

tusks (TUHSKS) long, pointed teeth; often used for fighting or digging

wallows (WAHL-ohz) muddy areas where pigs go to cool off

Bibliography

Downes, Lawrence. "Hunting Pesky Pigs in Paradise." *The New York Times* (May 15, 2013).

Mayer, John J., and I. Lehr Brisbin Jr. *Wild Pigs in the United States: Their History, Comparative Morphology, and Current Status*. Athens, GA: University of Georgia Press (2008).

Morthland, John. "A Plague of Pigs in Texas." *Smithsonianmag.com* (January 2011).

Stegemann, Eileen. "Pigs Gone Wild: Feral Swine Threaten New York State." *New York State Conservationist* (October 2012).

Read More

Aronin, Miriam. *Florida's Burmese Pythons: Squeezing the Everglades (They Don't Belong: Tracking Invasive Species)*. New York: Bearport (2016).

Collard, Sneed B. III. *Science Warriors: The Battle Against Invasive Species*. Boston: Houghton Mifflin (2008).

Quinlan, Julia J. *Wild Boars (Ferocious Fighting Animals)*. New York: PowerKids Press (2013).

Learn More Online

To learn more about feral pigs, visit
www.bearportpublishing.com/TheyDontBelong

Index

About the Author

Kevin Blake lives in Providence, Rhode Island—the capital of one of the few states without feral pigs—with his wife, Melissa, and son, Sam. This is his ninth book for kids.

BOOK CHARGING CARD

Accession No. _____ Call No. _____

Author _____

Title _____

| | Borrower's Name | |